THE CONCISE HISTORIES OF **DEVON**

# DEVON AND THE SECOND WORLD WAR

THE CONCISE HISTORIES OF **DEVON**

THE MINT PRESS

# DEVON AND THE SECOND WORLD WAR

NICK SMART

First published in Great Britain by The Mint Press, 2003

ISBN 1-903356-29-6

Cataloguing in Publication Data
CIP record for this title is available from the British Library


The Mint Press
18 The Mint
Exeter, Devon
England EX4 3BL

Cover and text design by Delphine Jones

Main cover illustration: Private Collection

Coin: Farthing, 1947 (by courtesy of Exeter Museums Service)

Printed and bound in Great Britain
by Short Run Press Ltd, Exeter.

# CONTENTS

# DEVON
## AND THE
# SECOND WORLD
# WAR

The days were getting noticeably shorter. But though the turning leaves and heavy morning dews bore the unmistakable signs of autumn, the holiday season was still in full-swing at the beginning of September 1939. The summer had been fine. Few Devon farmers would admit as much, but the harvest promised well. The holiday trade prospered. Continuing good weather, and the common realization that with general war in Europe imminent the time left for frivolous diversion was short, led to a spate of late bookings in the seaside towns.

The prospect of war was not welcome, but the population was sufficiently in-tune with the government to accept it if it came. Neville Chamberlain had learned the hard way not to trust Hitler's word, and - something of a political achievement - had managed to translate his personal sense of betrayal into a generally shared mood. When news of Molotov and Ribbentrop's notorious non-aggression pact emerged, few hankered after a second Munich. Fewer still wished to renege on Britain's commitment to defend Hitler's next intended victim,

Poland. There was no flagwaving, still less much practical thought given to quite how the threatened Poles might be helped. But, convinced that there were evil things they would be called on to fight against, the people of Devon, in common with the rest of the population, were prepared to do what they were told was necessary. Newspapers were studied, and wireless news bulletins listened to intently. On the first day of September Germany invaded Poland. That day and the next the people braced themselves for a declaration of war on Germany

Fierce thunderstorms deluged London and southern England on the night of 2 September. But everywhere, next morning, a Sunday, was bathed in fine sunshine.

Unaware of the rough treatment the government front bench had received in the House of Commons the previous evening, wireless listeners, forewarned by solemn BBC announcers that the prime minister would broadcast at 11.15 a.m., waited by their sets. Church attendance was low that morning. Most people knew, or sensed, what Chamberlain would say. There was little feeling of surprise of shock. Instead there was widespread sympathy for the old man, as, in his tired weary voice, he lamented how everything he had worked for had crashed in ruins. The need to listen-in, as though performing an act of witness, was the first collective British memory of the outbreak of what is remembered as the Second World War.

Reaction in Devon was as elsewhere. The mayor of Barnstaple, just back from a visit to the United States, spoke of the town's steadfastness, while the local paper reported a rush of weddings and, as an alleged means of protecting windows from bomb-blast, carried prominent advertisements for distemper. In Plymouth, as in London, the wail of the air raid sirens - a false alarm - pierced the air. Barrage balloons were hoisted to float lazily in the still air. In less jittery Exmouth the hire of deckchairs went on uninterrupted, though next morning council workers descended on the beach and began the job of filling 49,000 sandbags.

A nation girding itself up for war can be made to appear impressive over the wireless. All manner of special measures were announced in the King's name. Places of entertainment were temporarily closed. While the call-up of men to the services was gradual, civil defence measures, including the blackout, were imposed before the declaration of war. Householders were advised to keep buckets of water and sand handy and, if possible, to invest in a stirrup-pump. Devon, accustomed to city-dwelling summer visitors, was already receiving migrants whose motives for travel had less to do with pleasure than safety. These were the evacuees; those who heeded the government's advice that Britain's industrial cities were vulnerable to air attack, and moved to areas the bombers would be less likely to reach. The well-to-do tended to make their own arrangements. Some boarding schools did the same. The Sun Alliance Assurance Company had already transferred to Torquay. The newsreel company, Gaumont, re-located itself to Crediton. For months past the 'properties wanted' columns of Devon newspapers had been filled with hopefully worded enquiries about houses or flats to let. Those less well-off were encouraged to surrender themselves to the dictates of the government's evacuation scheme, planning for which had been undertaken by the ministry of health over the previous two years.

Government contingency planning assumed that Germany would take the offensive and mount a sustained aerial assault on Britain's cities. London, well within operational range, the seat of government and the home of one-fifth of the population, was considered the most likely target. Estimating the number of aircraft the Germans had at their disposal, and calculating that every ton of high explosive dropped in a built up area would inflict 50 casualties, the authorities had produced an equation which, by any standard, was apocalyptic. Believing the Luftwaffe was capable of a two-month long sustained assault, as many as 600,000 fatalities were expected with a further 1,200,000 casualties. Confronted with this grim prospect the government considered it vital to thin-out the urban population and, as an emergency measure, send as many 'inactive' people as possible (principally children, nursing mothers and the disabled) to the relative safety of the provinces. The intention, to save life and alleviate mass air-raid induced panic, was to reduce the population of the big cities by one-third. This meant moving upwards of four million people from areas of highest risk.

Because considered beyond the effective range of enemy aircraft, and possessing a great deal of out-of season housing stock, Devon loomed large in government pre-war planning as a reception area for London evacuees. For their part the county authorities prepared themselves as best they could for the expected influx. A gesture towards the military importance of Plymouth's naval base and dockyard, resulted in the city being designated a neutral (ie non-receiving) area, though elsewhere in the county very large numbers were expected. A pre-war 'billeting survey' had estimated that even allowing for 50,000 'voluntary' transfers to Devon, there was still accommodation available for some 200,000 evacuees under the government's 'official' scheme.

In the event this estimate, submitted to the ministry of health with an accompanying request for 30,000 mattresses and 80,000 blankets, bore little relation to what actually happened. The rate of arrival, as it turned out, did not approach the level expected and, in common with other south-western counties, Devon hosted many more 'voluntary' evacuees than the 'unexpectedly low' numbers who came (still less stayed) under the 'official' scheme. This, perhaps, was just as well. It meant that billeting officers seldom had to use the compulsory powers vested in them. Nevertheless even at its reduced level of intensity, the exodus from the cities posed sufficient problems for local authorities, the newly formed Women's Voluntary Service (WVS) and householders paid 10s and 6d a week to act as 'foster parents' for an unaccompanied child.

It is fashionable to deride the failings

of the 1939 evacuation. That government
got its sums so wrong in the first place,
grossly exaggerating the numbers
participating in its 'official' scheme, is one
obvious criticism. It seems funny now, but
the bewilderment of the reception
committee gathered on Paignton station
platform to greet 400 evacuees must have
been palpable when an empty train
arrived. But where transfers were effected
they were often insensitively managed.
Schools were needlessly broken-up,
brothers and sisters separated and
mothers reduced to anxious dependency.
The absence of system caused much
distress. There were neither medical
checks, facilities for the disabled, nor
maternity provision for expectant

mothers. The image of middle-class selfishness, of rich women moving into Sidmouth hotels and there, installed for the duration, downing their cocktails and 'doing a bit of knitting for the troops', contrasts sharply with descriptions of the malnourished poverty of so many of the 'official' evacuees. The fate of hungry, dishevelled and demoralized children deposited on a blacked-out Totnes station platform, and there 'howling miserably' as they were shunted around and bargained over by billeting officers and potential foster parents, contributes to what has become a kind of folk-memory of the phoney war. At a time when all the sensations of war were present, except the fighting, grumbling took over. The bedwetting, lice-ridden evacuee child, 'sewn-in' for the winter by a sluttish mother, became a kind of national symbol.

Many foster-parents, aghast at the state of their plimsoll-shod unaccompanied charges, paid for shoes out of their own money. The extended run of the 1939 Starcross pantomime, put on by Southwark Central School, suggests that the county had its share of Mr Toms. But for every kind act there was, it has to be said, much resentment, ill-feeling and homesickness. Working class Londoners did not necessarily take to the pace of life in dear old Devon. Those who had never seen a cow before were not always impressed upon introduction and, a constant source of bafflement to health officials, evacuee children did not automatically grow or put on weight. Moreover there were plenty of locals quick to criticize the ingratitude and dirty ways of the incomers. Perhaps some were grateful to be billeted in one of the more picturesque parts of the country, but others recoiled from the primitive facilities of rural life. Being cast adrift, miles from anywhere, amidst remarkably incestuous communities of near paupers was no joke. Unsurprisingly the drift back to the cities began almost as soon as the first evacuees arrived. By the end of September 1939, the ministry of health's returns on the number removed to Devon estimated that 70,000 people had transferred themselves voluntarily, whereas a bare 10,000 - a mere five per cent of the anticipated total - remained in the county under the 'official' scheme.

This did not mean that Devon became a haven for the well-to do, or merely acted as a reception area for those who had only to step into their cars and buy their way to safety. The 1939 evacuation may not have worked especially well, but it is a mistake to regard it as a sort of census on the condition of England at the end of the 1930s. It was an emergency measure not a social experiment in seeing how the classes and the masses mixed. The gulf between rich and poor, haves and have nots, may have been vividly exposed, but the scheme itself can hardly be blamed for causing such divisions. Nor was evacuation unnecessary. Contrary to expectation the war was a year old before the bombing of British cities began in earnest, but it had not been foolish for the authorities to rehearse static defence measures against that eventuality. When the bombers did come, in the late summer of 1940, the war had entered a different phase. With Britain's strategic situation so suddenly perilous, evacuation began anew. It was as well that the exercise had been put through its dummy-run.

In a wider sense the 1939 evacuation is held up as an example, almost a metaphor, of the kind of fumbling administrative incompetence supposedly so characteristic during the months of the phoney war. At a time when government restrictions seemed unnecessarily onerous, and when the blackout was claiming more victims than enemy action, the scheme is made to represent the social side of a nation not especially united, militarily ill-equipped and, to boot, psychologically unprepared for 'total war'. As such it is linked to the assumed half-heartedness and complacency of the Chamberlain wartime administration. There is little justice in this. With no bombs falling it was as natural for evacuees to make for home as it was to resent the obtrusiveness of officialdom. The coal shortage of that harsh winter added to the level of complaint, and, such sensible measures as food rationing and putting the clocks forward in February so

as to gain an extra hour's daylight and,
effectively abandon GMT for the
duration, were heavily criticized. That few
bothered to carry their gasmasks was,
then, officially frowned upon. Later in the
war the same neglectful habit was
interpreted as a sign of high morale.

Nobody could predict how this
strange war would develop. Even had
there been more offensive action against
the German Westwall, or had the RAF
dropped bombs over Germany by night
instead of the notorious leaflets, Hitler's
timetable for his Blitzkrieg offensive in
the west would not have been altered.
When that came in May 1940, of course,
with Belgium, Holland and France
overrun and defeated in less than six

weeks, all the government's confident announcements about the war proceeding according to plan were exposed as humbug. It was Chamberlain not Hitler who had so evidently 'missed the bus'. Nevertheless, not everything that was established in the first months of the war was phoney. The wireless sounded the same wherever it was listened to. The BBC's It's That Man Again ('ITMA') comedy show, first broadcast from Bristol in September 1939, became a lasting wartime favourite. Devonians, like everybody else, 'enjoyed the novelty of being cajoled and hectored' by William Joyce ('Lord Haw-Haw') in their own sitting rooms'. Imitating Joyce's 'Jairmany calling' nasal whine became, in a small way, a mechanism for coping. As the ITMA catch-phrase had it, 'It's being so cheerful as keeps me going'.

Perhaps it was as well such innocent un-martial pleasures took root early; there being little point in pondering too hard the horrors lying ahead. With so little war news to report, it is difficult to know how any government could have abolished the sense of boredom that set in during the winter of 1939-40. The notion that Chamberlain failed miserably as war leader is, understandably, a foundation stone in the myth of Churchill as 'national saviour'. That the changeover was effected with such perfect timing meant that the nation's darkest hour was turned seamlessly into the finest. The coalition government Churchill led from May 1940 did, after all, preside over what became known as the 'people's war'. But Churchill, whether he created or simply reflected, a galvanic sense of collective purpose after the strategic catastrophe of the fall of France, did not, for all his inspiring speeches, quite create a coalition of the British people. The snobberies and social frictions of the phoney war were not eradicated simply because the war map looked bleak. The country stood alone in the summer of 1940. Churchill's history came to meet him in his Battle of Britain. But however swift the turnaround, from complacency to backs-to-the wall defiance, the people who grumbled over shortages or who evaded their billeting responsibilities were the same as those who served as fire-watchers, ran mobile kitchens for the WVS or who flocked to join the Local Defence Volunteers - the Home Guard.

The summer of 1940 was the time to be alive. Those were the heroic days. It was as though an emotional fund was established; an account in which the nation's reserves of courage, fortitude and cheerfulness were stored. This was as well, for over the next four-odd years of war there were to be many withdrawals. As, until the end of 1942, the Germans seemed to win victories whenever and wherever they struck, and as shortages began to bite, the civic fabric of Britain took on an increasingly dowdy look.

Moments of danger or excitement were surrounded by austere monotony. The country subsisted on its emotional capital. This generally sufficed. Children collected scrap metal and sorted waste. Citizens were urged to 'make do and mend, subscribe to war-related good causes, and 'dig for victory'. There were allotments, Mr. Middleton offered gardening tips over the wireless, and Devon's first 'pig club' was, allegedly, founded in Salcombe. For all the emphasis on state direction, the Second World War on the home front was, in many ways, the golden age of the voluntary organization. Charity was real enough. Though the face Britain presented to the world was proud and positive, there was a general slide into genteel poverty. Beer was weakened in strength, while alcohol consumption increased significantly. Smoking among adults became near universal. More women worked, but if leisure consisted of a visit to the cinema or an evening in a shabby taproom, the lack of alternative outlets for disposable income served to keep female emancipation in check.

# CHANGES
### OF
# ADDRESS

Amidst all this there was movement. Geographic mobility characterized life in the Second World War. Dreary hours waiting for trains in blacked out stations became the common lot. Likened to a 'demented cistern' forever draining and filling with water, Devon's social identity changed. Beforehand an inhabitant of Chagford might never have travelled to Exeter. Under wartime conditions only the aged or the infirm were left to rejoice in their lifelong provincial ignorance. Neighbourliness had to take a different turn now that living with strangers was the norm. The thousands of changes of address blurred distinctions between host and guest, 'local' and 'incomer'. An ever-larger transient population added to the mix. Quite what this meant in terms of lasting social change, is difficult to judge. Reaction varied. The Okehampton housewife who demanded compensation from the council for children 'imposed' on her, and who 'had never received elementary training in sanitary decency', represented one side of the coin. Enquiries from evacuee foster parents, impressive in their number and in every case deeply moving, submitted to local councils concerning procedures for adoption, was the other. As the movement of civilians and service personnel into the coastal towns ebbed and flowed, leading, as one writer to the Exmouth Journal described, 'to a calamitous decline in traditions of respect for persons and property', it was difficult, though not impossible to retain the old exclusivities. In rural mid-Devon the Home Guard was, from the start, officered by members of the local hunt. Having battled with their consciences over the ethics of fox-hunting in wartime, the arrival of LDV armlets and the spectre of enemy parachutists provided an immediate raison d'être.

Licensed to 'work the moor' in the King's name, the 6th. Battalion of the Devonshires, as it became, might have started with 48 rifles among 402 men, but it kept its hounds.

Not the smallest consequence of the fall of France in June 1940 was that with Britain's air defences outflanked, Devon was now well within the effective range of German aircraft based in northern and western France. This brought danger not only to native Devonians but to the colony of Belgian fishermen settled in Brixham, the 'little France' established in Plymouth, and for those exiled Channel islanders accommodated in Dartmouth and Torquay. Those who, whether as internees or prisoners of war, were housed in former holiday camps in Paignton and Seaton also found themselves in the front line. Amidst all this movement, roles were sometimes reversed. Air-raids turned hosts into guests, as bombed-out victims of first the Plymouth and then the Exeter blitz sought sanctuary in surrounding towns and villages. Beaches were wired-off and mined. Coastal batteries were established at river mouths. A 'stop line' of concrete pillboxes spread north from Axmouth, while squads of labourers (often Irish) created aerodromes from farmland. Even as the invasion scare was at its height, thousands of troops passed through the vast army training camps near Okehampton and at Dalditch on Woodbury Common.

Then, of course, there were the
Americans. Their 'friendly invasion'
began with the US Navy Air Force taking
over Dunkenswell aerodrome in late 1942.
Soon nearby Upottery was made over to
the USAAF. The pace quickened from
mid-1943 when American soldiers arrived
to prepare for the opening of the 'second
front'. Devon became a training ground
and depot for the US army. A large tract
of coastline around Woolacombe was
turned into a practice assault centre, and
American engineers, in providing
themselves with shower facilities, gifted
Braunton with a new water system. By the
spring of 1944, the physical impact of the
Americans reached its peak. Added to the
hutted camps around Tavistock, and great

pre-invasion tented enclosures above
Plymouth and around Torquay, there was
the US Navy's vast ninety-acre depot at
Exeter. Best known, perhaps, was the
giving over of much of the South Hams to
the US Army from November 1943. Eight
villages were evacuated in their entirety to
make way for a battle school in which,
using Slapton Sands as their simulated
landfall, American troops rehearsed
landing on beaches not too dissimilar
from those they would attack in earnest in
June 1944. It was off Slapton, incidentally,
where a practice amphibious exercise
went terribly wrong some six weeks before
D-Day. As is now well-documented,
German E-boats were able to slip though
the escort screen at night and attack

troop-laden landing craft in Lyme Bay
with devastating force.

Devon roads creaked under the strain
and Dartmoor was much tramped-over by
American soldiers. However not many
stayed for any length of time. Plymouth,
Dartmouth, Salcombe and Brixham
served as embarkation ports for operation
Neptune (the transportation and assault
phase of the invasion of Normandy) thus
thousands of troops were funnelled
through the county on their way to
France. Two assault wave formations, the
4th and 29th infantry divisions, had taken
up residence. But when they left, and the
theatre of operations moved eastwards,
the headquarters in Tavistock and
Tiverton were dismantled. Thereafter the

American presence in Devon declined markedly.

Nevertheless, the Americans left their mark. It seems that the old cliché about them being over-paid, over sexed and over-here, applied as much to Devon as it did anywhere else. Locals worn down by four years of wartime deprivation gawped in fascination at these young men exhibiting their own exotic sense of cool. They had money in their pockets and access to undreamed of material 'goodies'. Romantic attachments, whether induced through drink, the bait of chewing gum and nylons, or the thrill of jitterbugging, were frequent. 'We felt like queens' recalled an Exmouth woman. It was no time to be gay. Americans, like everybody else got bored. With leisure time consisting in the main of wandering aimlessly around in groups, sex, more the discussion of it than the act, assumed the dimensions of a territorial imperative. Men, ostensibly on the same side, fought each other in wartime Devon, and as often as not it was women, or a presumed right of access to them, who were the cause. The six-month jail sentences handed to the South Molton man for attacking an American who had 'fancy ways with the girls', was, doubtless intended as exemplary. But the police were usually powerless to prevent fights between racially segregated American servicemen from spilling into the streets. The situation got so bad that the authorities of

Newton Abbot negotiated a system barring 'colored' American units from visiting the town on the same evenings as their 'white' comrades-in-arms. This may have been a prudent means of managing sexually-stoked racial antagonisms, though what it says about the delights of Newton Abbot night life remains obscure. The notorious armed street battles waged by black and white American soldiers, like the one that raged over the Tamar in Launceston one Saturday night in September 1943, appear to have passed Devon by.

Having added their splash of colour to an otherwise pinched and gloomy wartime scene, the Americans departed. They left a wrecked South Hams, a lot of hutted camps, some babies, and, doubtless, a few broken-hearts. A legacy, so the stories go, was tons of surplus-to-requirement military equipment buried in pits. Devonians brushed themselves off and carried on as normal. A vivid though transient chapter in the wartime history of the county moved quietly to a close.

# ENEMY
# ACTION

A peculiar partisanship often afflicts those who write county histories. It sometimes leads them down strange avenues of reasoning. Thus a tenaciously held belief in distinctness has led to a number of dubious assertions about the 'unequalled diverse combination of events and factors' that made up the experience of Devon at war. Claimed as 'arguably the most military active county in the United

Kingdom', a tradition stretching back to Drake is invoked, and an enormous amount of energy poured into sustaining Devon's historic invasion-resisting role. It is as though the history of every shell fired or bombed dropped on Devon soil has had its history plotted. Yet though to an extent understandable, there is something blinkered about this parochial search for superlatives. Even if we had the means of measuring the extent of enemy action over Devon as opposed to, say, Merseyside, there must be reservations about the object of such study. Boasting Devon's pride of place in terms of wartime sacrifice and destruction belongs to the school playground. To chronicle suffering is one thing, to presume uniqueness is another.

As the home port of so many naval ships, Plymouth was the base from which the south western approaches were guarded. When aircraft carriers were withdrawn from picket-duty after the loss of the Courageous in September 1939, RAF Coastal Command's role in convoy protection increased. More aerodromes were built in Cornwall and Devon, and more aircraft flew from them. Later in the war more intense air and naval action was taken against enemy traffic in the Channel and, as the range of aircraft increased, patrol activity extended to the Bay of Biscay. British and American Devon-based squadrons also attacked U-boat bases with increasing, though seldom effective, frequency.

As a platform for operations Devon attracted the attention of the Germans across the Channel. Yet, contrary to what is sometimes implied, it is unlikely that German military leaders pondered their maps and concluded that the torso and neck of the south west peninsular, was their key to victory. The county featured in enemy strategic thinking, but was not the object of strategy. For four years of war Devon was easily within the Luftwaffe's range. For the first two of these the Germans, holding the initiative in the air, could regard the night skies as their own.

The Luftwaffe's two-year long bombing offensive against Britain was under-resourced, but in-so-far as it was strategically driven, attacking Devon targets was not patternless. Exeter, famously, was heavily bombed in two night raids in the spring of 1942. The city, harmless and defenceless, was in common with York, Bath, Norwich and Canterbury, made victim of the so-called Baedeker series of raids which, at the time, were said to have no object other than the destruction of ancient monuments. Latterly the idea that these raids were ordered as reprisal for the RAF's fire-bombing of Lübeck has gained currency, and it has even been suggested that they were delivered as a kind of coded message; a last-gasp attempt to persuade the British to limit aerial warfare and forgo a bombing offensive of their own. A simpler and more likely explanation is that the Germans reasoned cities like Exeter would be less heavily defended than industrial centres and calculated that a depleted bomber force would inflict heavy damage for little loss.

If so they were correct. The centre of Exeter was very heavily bombed. Some 200 people were killed, and the destruction of many Georgian buildings, Bedford Circus in particular, is still recalled as a tragedy. Though few, it seems mourn the levelling of the west quarter's slums, the standard anti-modernist sideswipe has it that the city, 'lost its heart and found a reinforced concrete transplant'. For all that, images of the medieval Cathedral, surviving battered but unbowed amidst the surrounding ruins, have become the west-country's equivalent of those pictures of a defiant St. Paul's, standing amidst the wreck of the City of London.

Plymouth may have had fewer architectural gems than Exeter. It was, and is, a rougher place. But in the suffering and destruction stakes county historians afford Plymouth the palm. Deemed 'size for size' the most heavily bombed of all British cities, there are many detailed accounts of its blitz. Descriptions are full of sympathy for the victims, though the tendency to promote the place as the brightest beleaguered citadel of courage in the land is unnecessary. As unnecessary is the way the antics of that most self-advertizing, and usually plumb silly politician, the MP for Sutton, Lady Astor, are woven into the story. A strange woman, her husband, Lord Astor, the Lord Mayor for most of the war years, usually gets an honourable mention. Often ill, he at least had the sense to operate in a lower key.

Paying deference to Lady Astor's cartwheel-turning, dancing on the Hoe stunts, county historians are fascinated by the Plymouth blitz. Unlike Malta the city did not receive a medal, though plenty say it should have done, if only because, in common with the George Cross island, obsolete Gladiator biplanes provided defence. But heroic suffering was a commonplace in the Second World War, and appalling though Plymouth's ordeal was it is as well, perhaps, to remember that the traffic was not one way. More civilians were killed by allied air-raids on one German city, Dresden in 1945, than died in Britain as a result of enemy air activity over the entire course of the war.

Considered too far off to matter, Plymouth's defences in 1941 were as 'sketchy' as they had been in 1940. Elementary precautions, like evacuating schoolchildren, could have been undertaken beforehand, and government slowness - local as well as central - in applying what had been learned from other cities' experience of civil defence and post-raid maintenance of essential services, does seem, in retrospect, to have been negligent. Whatever else Plymouth

represented in wartime it was, as seems
obvious now, a legitimate military target

Cum-uppance came in the spring of
1941; a depressing period. The dominions
were solid, and the financial lifeline
provided by lease-lend arrangements with
the United States was vital. But the war
seemed unremittingly to be going
Germany's way. As the shipping situation
grew more serious, German bombers
ranged over Britain by night almost at will.
In the new year of 1941 their attention
shifted to provincial centres, in particular
to the Atlantic facing ports which handled
the bulk of maritime trade. Bristol,
Clydebank and Liverpool had already
suffered grievously, but Plymouth, thus
far, had led something of a charmed life.

With little merchant shipping passing through its port, the city's inhabitants may have felt that but for the odd stray raider they would be left alone. They were wrong. However lowly placed on the Germans' list of provincial military targets, the importance of its naval base and dockyard, coupled to its ease of location, ensured that Plymouth was not forgotten.

On the night of 20 March 1941, just hours after a royal visit, the Plymouth blitz began. The scale of the attack that night and the next was unprecedented. The city centre was wiped out. The devastation was appalling. More than 300 civilians were killed and the glow from the fires could be seen thirty miles away. In an unplanned but unstoppable way thousands of people trekked out of the city at dusk seeking safety in the surrounding countryside. Defences - both civil and military - were overwhelmed. At the time and after the authorities were much criticized for their inability to cope, but at that stage in the war there was little effective defence against night bombers able to reach a target which, on moonlit nights, stood-out on a well-etched coastline. High explosives cut the water mains and incendiaries completed the devastation. This was bad. But the twist to the Plymouth blitz was worse. Whether pre-planned or not, the Luftwaffe stumbled on a tactic that Bomber Command was later to hone to dreadful perfection. This was to bomb a target, leave it substantially alone for a few weeks - while sending a few aircraft over to create air-raid alerts and thus sustain the cycle of fear - then return in devastating force. Kept awake at night with nerves on end over the first three weeks of April, Plymouthians suffered the consequences of the Luftwaffe's return at the end of the month. The coup de grace was clinically delivered.

In this second phase of the attack the built environment of central Plymouth, Stonehouse and much of Devonport simply ceased to exist. The dockyard was badly hit. Ship-repair equipment melted in the heat. Medical stores were incinerated. Naval and marine barracks were gutted by fire. After five heavy raids

in nine nights, civic administration all but
collapsed. At one stage more than 2,000
separate fires raged. Fire crews racing to
help from afar afield as Swindon often
found that the couplings on their hoses
would not fit the Plymouth hydrants.
Though casualty figures for the services
were not released, more than 600 civilians
were killed. 3,000 were injured and over
40,000 rendered temporarily homeless.
There was breakdown. No shops, no
water, no gas, no protection. The only
service to respond with quick sensitivity to
the disaster was, it seems, the public
assistance board. While looters lurked
behind, thousands trekked out of the city
on a nightly basis. Improvised rest centres
in surrounding villages were swamped,

and many caught what sleep they could in quarry tunnels, hayricks or on open moorland. The resident population dropped, officially, from 208,000 to 127,000. For a while Plymouth was cordoned off. The local newspapers, removed to Tavistock for printing spoke only of the courage of the people. It seemed to matter to the Western Morning News that Plymouth had assumed the 'mantle of Coventry'.

Herbert Morrison, the minister for Home Security, thought otherwise. Privy to home intelligence reports indicating that the mood of the people was not so much defeatist as defeated, he concluded that morale in Plymouth had gone, and, with a touch of cockney arrogance,

wondered how much more pounding
provincial centres could take. Churchill,
touring the wrecked city in an open car,
and receiving the ragged cheers of
scattered onlookers called forth by police
loudspeaker vans, publicly wept. Privately
he confided that he 'had never seen the
like'. Plymothians used to the patience of
poverty were by now rendered
superstitious of VIP presence. They
thought news of the prime minister's visit
would bring more bombs raining down
on them. Such was the Plymouth blitz.

But for the German invasion of the
Soviet Union in June 1941 there probably
would have been more heavy raids. But
when the strength of the Luftwaffe was
deployed far to the east, enemy air activity

over British skies was reduced. It did not cease altogether. The Baedeker raids after all, took place in the early summer of 1942, and sporadic attacks on Plymouth continued into 1944. Devon aerodromes remained vulnerable, and the RAF base at Chivenor, near Barnstaple, seems to have been a favourite target for German fighter-bombers. Though the county was spared the flying-bomb and V1 rocket attacks of 1944-5, south Devon towns received their fair share of daylight 'tip and run' raids over the next three years of war.

But as the dust settled on a destroyed Plymouth in the early summer of 1941 people could not know that, in scale at least, the worst of the bombing was over. Reaction was double-edged. At one level, as is often said, lessons learned included the need for systematic evacuation plans and a more rapid and coordinated post-raid response to the need for food, shelter and ready cash. The odd 'tenner-in-hand', it seems, worked wonders for the bombed-out, bereaved and demoralized citizen. A national fire service was created after the Plymouth blitz. Characteristically, though wrongly, Lady Astor claimed credit for this administrative reform.

At another level the desire for vengeance was strong. The Appledore shipyard workers who lined the quay threatening to lynch German airmen brought ashore may not have been typical, but the popular wish to repay them for what had been done to us had a strong bearing on future war strategy. To those ministers and their advisers who were attracted to the air-power theorists, the advocates of the 'knock-out blow' approach to strategic bombing, the example before them - of Plymouth destroyed - seemed to prove their point. In public politicians praised the city's courage and steadfastness. But behind the closed doors of Whitehall and, more especially, Bomber Command H.Q. in High Wycombe, the idea that the people's morale had cracked took root. The image of panic-stricken trekkers - a defeated rabble - appalled and intrigued in equal measure. If Plymouth showed that no civilian population could endure sustained aerial bombardment, how would the Germans respond once subjected to the same treatment?

Of the two contending fictions, that the bombed-out people of Plymouth retained a 'we can take it' cheerfulness, set against stories of civic breakdown, and mass absenteeism, the government borrowed more from the latter. Ministers, digesting reports of Plymouth's devastation in May 1941 were, at the same time, receiving glum accounts of the RAF's inability to locate and bomb military targets in Germany. Precision-bombing, it was found, was not working. On moonless nights, as the Butt report later revealed, fewer than one-fifth of aircraft despatched reached the target area, and less than 10 per cent of bombs

dropped fell within five miles of a target.
The solution, and the fate of Plymouth
was cited in support, was 'area' bombing.
Henceforth Bomber Command would not
trouble over 'military targets'. Instead it
would attack the morale of German
civilian workers by 'de-housing' them.
The means were to hand. Whereas the
type of bomber the Germans used to
attack Plymouth had a range of 1,500
miles carrying a bomb-load of 8,000 lbs,
the four-engined 'heavies' beginning to
roll off British production lines could fly
for 2,500 miles with a payload nearly three
times as heavy.

The dreadful phoenix that rose from
the ashes of the Plymouth blitz was an
empowered Bomber Command. The

1,000 bomber raid; the carpeting of cities like Cologne with high explosive and incendiaries, enacted by 'Bomber' Harris from May 1942, became the means by which the fight was carried to the enemy. This, the so-called strategic bombing offensive was, for all the dedication and heroism of the aircrews involved, both a crime and a mistake. Two wrongs, as we used to be taught in primary school, seldom make a right. The systematic destruction of German cities was hideously expensive. Apologists say it shortened the war. If it did it was at the cost of a lot of civilian lives.

By mid 1942 the terms of the war had changed dramatically. Britain was no longer alone. Though the U-boat menace remained, victory was now assured; a question of when, not if. This was the main theme, though one minor sub-plot was still to be worked out. This consisted of Luftwaffe 'tip and run' raids which were carried out till the spring of 1944. In the overall scheme of things they may have been no more than a nuisance, but as virtually every built up place from Seaton to Plymstock had at least one visitation from low-flying fighter-bombers, their impact on south Devon was considerable. Approaching in daylight and from seaward, they arrived without warning and were gone before any alarm was raised.

Kingsbridge and Teignmouth were attacked in this manner in early 1943.

Damage in Dartmouth persuaded the
authorities to move the cadets from the
Britannia naval college to Cheshire, and,
by a circuitous process of logic, install
WRNS girls and American engineers in
their stead. Torquay suffered severely. In
one incident the Palace Hotel, turned
into an RAF hospital, was wrecked. In
another 21 children and their Sunday
School teachers were killed when the St
Marychurch parish church received a
direct hit. Over in Exmouth the evacuated
schoolgirl, the sculptress to-be, Elisabeth
Frink, thought she was dead when, having
dived to the ground as German fighters
bombed and strafed the seafront, she rose
amidst the dust and smoke to behold the
trees festooned bizarrely with clothes.

Blast, having blown the windows of houses out, had taken with it the contents of bedroom wardrobes. A couple of hundred yards away in the town centre, 20 people were killed by a high explosive bomb. They had been waiting to catch a bus.

# PLOUGH UP

Attempts to affix a relationship of people to place are always difficult. Perhaps then, in the war years, there was, or could be said to be, a distinct Devonshire sensibility. For all that we might be persuaded to think there was, it is difficult, frankly, to discern one now. Perhaps this is the purpose historians serve; to sprinkle root propagation powder among those seeking to find an identity though the past. While the theme of this book has been movement; stressing change not continuity in wartime Devon, there are grounds nevertheless for claiming a degree of specialness. These do not lie in the realm of heroic suffering, but in terms of production - and in particular the production of food. For Devon farmers' contribution to the national war effort was considerable, and indeed, worthy of note.

In national terms there was something of an agricultural revolution during the war, and there is a firm empirical, or at any rate statistical, basis for saying that Devon was in the vanguard. Apart from anything else, with Yorkshire divided into its parts, Devon was the largest English or

Welsh county on the Ministry of
Agriculture's books, with over one million
acres of cultivated land making it the
largest agricultural production unit in the
land. The rural economy, so extensively
depressed before the onset of hostilities
was transformed in wartime. Farmers
today would have little difficulty
identifying with the pre-war scene; falling
profit margins, shedding labour and
letting more land pass out of cultivation.
Their trouble would be to recall the
wartime years of boom whereby, in the
process of producing more, farmers
enriched themselves.

At war's outset only some 30 per cent
by value of the food consumed in Britain
was home-produced. With some 23

million tons of food, animal feeding stuffs and fertilisers imported in 1938, the ministry of agriculture's wartime brief was clear. With the country having to pay its way, and with shipping space at a premium, imports would have to be drastically reduced. Moreover, given the need to restrict imported animal feeding stuffs, as well as the greater calorific value attached to crop-growing, the nation's diet would have to shift from meat to cereals and vegetables. Although the ministry was concerned to maintain milk supplies, its main effort was directed to expending livestock and promoting intensive arable farming. The ploughing up of grassland was, from the beginning, 'the key to war-time production policy'.

Many Devon farmers found themselves ill-placed to meet this imperative. With so much of the available land marginal or best-suited to permanent pasture, the conversion to arable farming required know-how, fertilizers, machinery and, a commodity that was in increasingly short supply as the war progressed, labour. Nevertheless the turnaround was significant and impressive. At war's outset, and discounting 300,000 moorland acres suitable only for rough-grazing, 720,000 acres of Devon farmland (65 per cent of the cultivated total) was devoted to permanent pasture. A further 220,000 acres (20 per cent of the total) was given over to rotational grasses, leaving a bare 15 per cent of the county's cultivated land to crop growing. Within a year the plough-up campaign had reduced the grassland acreage to 650,000 acres, (50 per cent) and increased crop acreage to 300,000 (27 per cent). Despite the necessity of avoiding soil exhaustion by, effectively, giving fields a rest under sowed grasses, the trend towards arable farming continued right through the war. By mid-1943 pasture had declined to 530,000 acres, (43 per cent) while 400,000 acres (38 per cent) had been brought directly under the plough. A further 100,000 acres were given over to rotation grasses.

Whereas nationally the great plough-up had an adverse affect on the rearing of livestock, Devon was something of an exception to the general rule. Pigs and poultry did decline significantly, such that by 1945, Devon pork and egg production was about half what it had been in 1939, but the county's dairy herd actually increased in size. This was achieved through flexible, and often quite subtle farming methods. Bracken clearing and liberal applications of lime brought thousands of acres of rough moorland pasture back into cultivation, and a system of rotation from cereals to grasses to pasture - ley farming as it was known - allowed for increased cropping, while keeping a substantial acreage constantly available for animal feeding stuffs. Despite considerable government requisitioning of land for military purposes, the acreage under cultivation in Devon increased year by year. By today's terms environmental good practice was thrown aside. Hedgerows were grubbed out and copses removed. Even the land in between trees in established orchards was ploughed. Crop and wheat acreage doubled by 1943. Onions virtually disappeared, but potato growing increased five-fold.

Many factors combined to effect this change. One was the £2 per acre ploughing subsidy offered to farmers from war's beginning. Another was a particularly active county war agricultural executive committees (CWAEC) which, made up in the main of 'respected local farmers and dignitaries' appointed by the ministry, prodded, advised and, under certain circumstances, compelled compliance with ministry instructions. With the state, in the shape the ministry of food, acting as a monopoly buyer, farmers could maximize production on the basis of guaranteed income and, for that little bit extra, there was always the black market to tap-into. Devon farmers may have had to 'fill in ten times more forms... than they were accustomed to' before the war, but - whether applying for subsidies to kill rats, erect silos or lay drains, they seemed to catch-on to the idea that officials had their uses. Between 1939 and 1945 agricultural net incomes quadrupled, rising at a faster rate than wages, salaries and profits in any other sector.

To read of the mechanization of British agriculture during the war years is to be reminded, at one level, of the propaganda surrounding collectivization in the Soviet Union. There was no five-year plan, as such and no peasant kulaks to be eradicated, but, assuming the veracity of British statistics, the war did for the horse and ushered-in the age of the tractor. Land army girls atop combine harvesters, or operating milking machines, became a kind of socialist realist icon of wartime British agriculture. Under the benevolent auspices of the ministry, the number of tractors on Devon farms, 1300 in 1939, grew to 3,000 in 1942, rising to 6,000 in 1944. Other types of farm machinery, ploughs, drills, and milking machines also saw significant increases.

Nationally the number of full-time farm workers declined slightly during the war, and though there was a small increase in Devon, the gross figures conceal considerable net change. In the early and middle phases of the war, when the call up of men to the forces was at its most intense, the agricultural workforce became heavily feminized. There were many more female part-time workers, and the contribution of the women's land army, at its peak strength of around 80,000 in 1943, was important. Some 'land girls' lived on the farms they worked, though increasingly they were based in hostels from which, in gangs, they were directed to jobs by the CWAEC. A training centre for these famously tough and non-squeamish women was set up at Whimple. But towards war's end the trend towards feminization halted, and then reversed. This, due in part, to the curtailment of land army recruitment, owed most to the discovery and exploitation of new source of labour power: prisoners of war.

No army command particularly liked having to devote space and resources to guarding prisoners, and southern command was for a long time successful in keeping PoWs out of its area. Camps for German prisoners were established in Holsworthy, Lydford and Beaworthy from 1942, and another was established in a former US army camp near Tiverton in late 1944. But gradually army resistance to guarding and feeding so many 'useless mouths' were overtaken by the ministry of agriculture's insatiable appetite for more workers. A reading of war office files shows how the initial web of regulations reflecting concerns over security and fraternization were first relaxed then dispensed with altogether, and offers some idea of how PoWs, especially Italians, came to feature ever more prominently in farming. In 1941 2,500 Italian prisoners were shipped from the middle east to help with the harvest. They were marched to and from work under guard. By 1943 there were 60,000 Italian PoWs working on British farms, and by 1945 (by which time their status had officially changed from 'prisoner' to 'cooperator') there were 130,000. Nobody bothered about security by then. Regarded as biddable, hard-working and, no doubt, fond of the ladies, many Italians lived on the farm. Many more, like 'land girls', were put up in CWAEC hostels. The Uffculme hostel housed 70 Italian quarry-workers. By war's end, with not a guard to be seen, there were some 6,000 Italians working in Devon agriculture.

It was in the immediate post-war years that the employment of former PoW agricultural labour reached its peak in Britain. By then many Germans had added to the numbers. Shipped back to Britain from North America, and still subject to military discipline, they were set to work prior to repatriation. Many, particularly those whose homes were in eastern Germany, stayed. Of all the exotic visitors to wartime Devon, the Americans, understandably, are the best remembered. They had money and glamour. Prisoners of war had neither. In status terms they were at the bottom of the heap. But compared to them the Americans were mere birds of passage. It is calculated that by 1945 food production in Britain - measured in terms of its calorific value - had increased by 91% in comparison with 1939. That it had done so was due, in no small measure, to prisoner of war labour power.

# ENDS
## AND
# BEGINNINGS

There was a certain symmetry to
Devon's war. It had begun quietly, and
it ended on a note of anti-climax. The
drama came in the middle years. By the
time the street parties were held in May
1945, all passion was spent. As weeds grew
on Plymouth bombsites, the Home Guard
was stood down and a 'dimout' replaced
the blackout. Rationing was as severe. A
threadbare down at heel Devon welcomed
peace and celebrated victory.

The idea prevails that British society changed during the war years. Common sense leads us to suppose it probably did. The destruction, disruption and dislocation of it all must have made an impact. What is odd though is the still prevalent belief that social change must have occurred (surely a most sensitive and difficult to define process, whether in peace or war) because otherwise the Labour party would not have won its famous victory in the 1945 general election. Yet whether people had discovered a taste for social justice or state welfare during the war, why a political event (an election) should be held up as proof or confirmation of a social process is, to this writer, something of a mystery.

But for all that, and offered very much in a for-what-it-is worth sense, some comment on Devon's non-contribution to the 1945 Labour landslide may be of interest.

It is the case that the three Plymouth constituencies 'went Labour'. This was not amazing. Drake was traditional Labour territory, and even in Lady Astor's Sutton (her husband, incidentally, had put his foot down and ordered her not to stand) Labour's challenge had always been strong. Michael Foot got in at Devonport displacing the talented, clever but by now back-numbered Leslie Hore-Belisha. Outside Plymouth though there was no change. George Lambert, a positive relic of Victorian times, was re-elected in South

Molton. Elsewhere in the county the electoral map remained, as it had been in the previous general election of 1935, blue. At one level there is no reason to query why it should not have done. At another it suggests that a Devonian conservatism of thought and habit still persisted despite, or maybe because of, all that had happened in the war.

# FURTHER READING

An obvious starting point is Gerald Walsey's *Devon's War 1939-45* (Exeter, 1994), though Robin Stane's *A History of Devon* (Chichester, 1986) is a useful introduction. For a refreshingly light-hearted approach, see Brian Powell's *Devon's Glorious Past* (Torquay, 1995).

There are lots of picture books. Books on the Exeter and Plymouth blitzes also abound. Geoff Worrall's *Target Exeter* (Stoke-on-Trent, 1983) has recently been joined by Peter Thomas' illustrated *Exeter Burning* (Tiverton, 2002). Walsey's *Blitz: An Account of Hitler's Aerial War over Plymouth* (Exeter, 1991) is fuller than Frank Wintle's *The Plymouth Blitz* (Truro, 1981). Ken Small's *The Forgotten Dead*

(London, 1998) tells the story of the Slapton Sands disaster of April 1944. Probably the best book on the Americans in Britain during the war is David Reynold's *Rich Relations: The American Occupation of Britain,* 1942-1945 (London, 1995).

*Farthing, 1947*
*(by courtesy of Exeter Museums Service)*

**Also available in the Concise Histories of Devon Series**

| | |
|---|---|
| *Roman Devon* | Malcolm Todd |
| *The Vikings and Devon* | Derek Gore |
| *Devon and the Civil War* | Mark Stoyle |
| *Cromwellian and Restoration Devon* | Ivan Roots |
| *Georgian Devon* | Jeremy Black |

*Also by* **The Mint Press**

**The Devon Engraved Series**

*Exeter Engraved: The Secular City* (2000)

*Exeter Engraved: The Cathedral, Churches, Chapels and Priories* (2001)

*Devon Country Houses and Gardens Engraved* (2001)

*Dartmoor Engraved* (2001)

**The Travellers' Tales Series**

*Exeter* (2000)

*East Devon* (2000)

*Cornwall* (2000)